To Margaret,

Petit Mal

JOHN W. SEXTON

POETRY

A WHITE HOUSE POETRY BOOK

Revival Press
Limerick - Ireland

First published in Ireland by
Revival Press
Moravia
Glenmore Avenue
Roxboro Road
Limerick
Ireland

www.revivalpress.ie

In association with the
White House Poets

www.myspace.com/thewhitehousepoets

Book design: Kelly Richards Printing, Limerick.
Cover painting 'Norseman in Ballinskelligs' by Aurelio Caminati.

Project editor: Dominic Taylor

ISBN No: 978-0-9554722-6-8

A CIP catalogue record for this book is available from The British Library.

For my brother
Peter

The hag in her bower at Rathmore
will trouble the children no more.
They've left crosses of sedge
in field and in hedge
and sleep safe in their dreams and snore.

Acknowledgements:
Many of the poems in this collection have previously appeared in the following journals:

The Burning Bush, The Cúirt Annual 2003, Cyphers, Equinox, The Illustrated Ape, Imagine, Incognito, Lumen, nthposition, Poetry Chaikhana, Poetry Ireland Review, Revival, Simply Haiku, The Shop, Southword, The Stony Thursday Book, Triptych Haiku, Wild Ireland and *World Haiku Review.*

Some also appear in the following anthologies:

Census **(7 Towers Publishing)** (edited by Sarah Lundberg), *Cúm* (edited by Moya Cannon), *In The Criminal's Cabinet* (edited by Val Stevenson and Todd Swift), *Microphone On* **(White House Press)** (edited by Dominic Taylor), *New Writing Cork 1999* (edited by Patrick Galvin), *Podium 2* (edited by Noel King), *Poems for Madrid* (edited by Todd Swift).

Song of Taliesin is based on the reconstructed prose version by Robert Graves and was originally published in *The Shop*.

Uncle Jack was broadcast as part of **The Living Word** on RTE Radio.

Mantra of the Awoken Powers, Silence and *Thief of Dreams* also feature on the cd *The Sons of Shiva*, with music by Hugh Cornwell (Track Records).

the streets beneath the ocean was recorded by *Cannery Row* and appears on their cd **No Homes** under the title **Underwater Girl** (vocals by Colin O'Sullivan, music by Bill Blizzard).

The essay *The Goddess Of Merciless Love* first appeared in **Poetry Ireland Review 68, Spring 2001** (edited by Biddy Jenkinson).

the little tea party was originally commissioned by Deborah Healy of **The Rowan Tree Gallery** to accompany their spring exhibition at the Sheen Falls Lodge 2004, and was first published in the exhibition catalogue. The poem was inspired by the work on display, which included paintings and sculpture by Cormac Boydell, Emma Corlett, Rebecca Durkin, Cian Hallissey, Deborah Healy, Joan Hodes, Con Kelleher, John Kingerlee, Joanna Kuper, Lili le Cain, Dermot McCarthy, Niall Naessens, Christopher O'Connor, Joop Smits, Charles Tyrrel and Marianne Wiersma.

My Granda as Lama Tensing won third prize in the **2004 Hiberno-English Poetry Competition** and first appeared in **The Hiberno-English Archive** (edited by Terence Patrick Dolan).

The Green Owl won the **Listowel Poetry Prize 2007** and first appeared in **The Listowel Writers' Week Winners Anthology 2007**.

A Concise Natural History was short-listed for **The Amergin Poetry Award 2007**.

The author wishes to thank Kate Kennelly & **Kerry County Council Arts Office** for granting him a bursary in 2007.

The author would also like to thank the Trustees of the **Patrick Kavanagh Trust** for the generous endowment of a **Patrick and Katherine Kavanagh Fellowship**, which enabled him to complete this book.

Contents

My Granda as Lama Tensing

Lama Tensing stops at the river and grasps his chest
his disciples panic, fuss around him,
                              but already his chest has opened
sparrows are exiting from the wound
twenty-five sparrows in all
the disciples count each single one
and every one of them made of smoke
as they swoop down into the grass
are absorbed by the earth

Lama Tensing Twenty-Five Sparrows
journeys through the bursting heart of the world
comes out through a wound in the yard
where my grandfather stands by the spigot
Oh Granda, you grasped your chest
                              and twenty-five sparrows flew out
but no one saw them for they were made of smoke
I'm only twelve, Granda, and too far away
I cannot hold you as you fall

I know only that the sparrows fly over the yard
over the galvanized roof of the shed
the feochadáns are ripening in the field
their spoked seeds floating up
each becomes the heart of a sparrow
and all is healed

the willowed grove

I went down to the willowed grove,
where the river troubles itself with stones,
and met a woman made of shadow
making herself a coat of thorns.

"Why do you clothe yourself in thorns,
O strange young woman of the darkest skin?"
"So that no man can touch my flesh,
only birds and insects enter in."

"O pretty young girl, you're as dark as space,
but your beauty outshines every star;
undress yourself of your thorny coat
and I'll be your lover without a care."

"You can't love me, you mortal man,
for I am ancient as the sea.
I was unborn before you were made,
and no man's love am I meant to be."

O I went down to the willowed grove,
where the river troubles itself with stones,
and met a woman made of shadow
making herself a coat of thorns.

Junior Infants And The Concept of Entropy

The Devil, Mrs. Hickey told the class,
had a name that meant The Prince of Light. But
because he had ideas of who he was,
God saw a problem and that light was snuffed.
Perhaps this subject roused inside my son
a child's first rough grasp of infinity;
he asked, "Dad, is God really Number One,
and is the Devil in the Trinity?"
I'd like to tell him that God is Not; or
darkness is the instrument of light; nought
is the origin of substance; error
the catalyst of right. But fear I'm caught.
When I was a kid ignorance was bliss;
I haven't travelled far to get to this.

the invisible horses

the invisible horses gallop through walls
immune to solidity they move through matter
sitting at your desk you are unaware of their passing
during the rush hour cars are blocked bumper to bumper
the traffic lights go green through red, green through red in mockery
the invisible horses slice through everything, are stopped by nothing
young children feel a breeze, turn their heads, pull at their mothers
the invisible horses plough through the city, relentless in their enigmatic pursuit
night falls, traffic becomes less, the streets grow quiet,
                              only the horses pass through
a drunkard staggering home feels something go through him, shivers
a police car moves slowly along the deserted streets, unaware of the tumult
the invisible horses gallop on, they are without number, infinite over the earth
they have been running since they were first imagined, their numbers increasing
the invisible horses gallop through walls, through cities, mountainsides
they run into the sea, out of the sea, pass each other in numberless thousands
they mass against each other over the seafloor, slow down only
                              at the greatest depths
there they pass through the foundations of the earth, moving in all directions
no part of the inner earth is without them, they pass through the core
in the depths of other oceans they emerge again,
                              pass others entering against them
nothing can stop them, they know no rest, never stop for breath, never sleep
no one can see them except in dreams where often they are glimpsed
once in a dream I mounted one, held on to his mane as he galloped on
he took me through cities, through armies of men,
                              through mountains and out again
the invisible horses amass in their countless numbers, their purpose inscrutable
never alive they can never die, they are infinite, infinite, infinite over the earth

in the near distance

rising high above the sweet factory was a tall brick chimney
as tall as any of the blocks of flats to the east
at the very top of the chimney was the word Maynards
the only thing that Maynards made as far as we knew were wine gums
but we couldn't work out what the chimney had to do with sweets

thick white smoke would pour out of it during the day
smoke so heavy that it had trouble rising into the air
and would usually just accumulate
                                into a bulbous cloud beside the chimney-mouth
from the school playground during afternoon sports we'd often see it
and wonder

a sickly smell like burnt treacle would waft through the streets around the school
it'd enter classroom windows and hang over the desks
once or twice, after school, we took a trek to the factory
but soon gave it up when we realised
that there were no sweets paving the road outside the gate

a tall brick wall topped with rusting spikes surrounded the factory
the whole place looked sinister and gave every kid in the school the creeps
I often wondered what made that thick smoke
imagined that black coal, sticky with bitumen, was an ingredient of the sweets
and never developed a taste for wine gums until well into my adult years

but oftentimes in winter when the fog would bind the factory smoke
we'd stand in the playground in the leaden mist
the sky fallen into our lives
and breathe the waste fumes of the sweet factory, our young tongues acrid
our minds opening up to the dullness of the world

Hymn

moon is caught
above the trees
owl cuts it free

sing praise to owl
sing praise
sing praise

owl rips darkness
from the sky
the stars come through

sing praise to owl
sing praise
sing praise

owl rescues mice
from boring lives
in the worthless grass

sing praise to owl
sing praise
sing praise

owl is dark
when the moon is dark
bright when it's bright

sing praise to owl
sing praise
sing praise

owl is death
to all not owl
owl is night

sing praise to owl
sing praise
sing praise

owl wraps the dead
in mourning shrouds
of mangled fur

sing praise to owl
sing praise
sing praise

the enchanted cowpat

with his foot he breaks a crusted cowcake
carries the secret over the moonlit meadow
and up the carpet of the stairs unknowingly
prints out sixty steps of greening toe-prints
and kicks off his shoes straight under the bed
falls down onto the mattress fully clothed
the moon still on above the trees he snores
as the shit on the rug turns on its heel
retraces itself down the sixty steps
walks itself out from every blade of grass
a scuttery foot-rise glinting silver
soft currency of green under moonbeams
back up the hill each step of turd untrod
resurrected whole while that fool still nods

Picasso's Rendering

Picasso says "and so and such and such   and so and so"
and and and   the translucent funnel of his mind
is darkened   by his black viscous thoughts
that soon will clog   the soft machinery of art
with brilliant light
and the minotaur comes
from the dark lake   with the virgin
in its arms, the blood from her thighs as dark
as the minotaur's thoughts
that soon will clog   the soft mythology of art
with brilliant light
and the thread that led the minotaur
to her innocent flesh
was unravelled from the towel
that absorbed her monthly blood
and the minotaur enters the labyrinth   of her body
to be absorbed by light
and the face of the minotaur   is the flat
tortoise face of Picasso, and he says
"and stones and more stones
and such and such and so and such
and so and such and such and so and so"
and the fragile machinery of our thoughts
are clogged with his.

the little tea party

invited to the little party

      seashells, bones & feathers dream themselves alive
        reinvent themselves into sea-urchin hedgehogs

a child dreams of an owl
      hidden in bolts of coloured cloth

a mountain leaves its shape in the fog
      a woman lifts the sky against her shoulder

in shallow rockpools
      seaweed inkstains a mermaid into life
        a man's dreaming faces emerge all at once

the shadows of trees form a bridge into night
      soft empires of sea kiss the land

lovers print snow-angels with their bodies
      write secret signs in frost

laughing crows hide in the chaos of dreams
      giants hug their knees and turn to stone
        a vase holds the outside in place
          while the inside sleeps untouched

an entire life is written down on a face
      an angel keeps the world safe in its mouth
        the king of the spotted dogs demands a bone

bluebells invent the colour blue
      the sea invents the sky
        the sky thinks of nothing but simply waits

As my mother casts cities asunder

Submerged in the sink the spoons lie like vessels with their engines cut
as mother slices the skin from a potato
On the skin are sprouted eyes like dull quartz, white cities of pale glass
that unfold onto the draining board
I watch the potato skin descend, berth
                            with a knock on the stainless steel top
and it looks like a brown island coming in to land,
                            its white jewel-like cities steering
their kingdom down from the sky
Piles of curled potato-peel accumulate beside the sink
I stare into the cities of potato eyes, imagine
                            their industrial furnaces burning
the thin juices of spudflesh
Then mum gathers the peelings into her hands and in a sudden the cities
are gone, and a furnace burns deep
                            in the foundations of her wedding ring
and her fingers wave in the air and the lightbulb flickers in the kitchen
for this is the world at six and at seven

Lao Tzu Notices Infinity For The First Time

Lao Tzu can count the scales on a snail's skin
can see the space   between the spokes
of a moving wheel
can see that space is greater   than the thing
that contains it
that the vessel is limited   by the extent of itself
whereas nothing has no self   to contain
has no limits, is as infinite   as the possibility of space
that the snail eases into
from the tight   twisting vessel of itself

The conference of witches at Venice

In the fire-garden the gardeners trimmed the burning lawns
with tears from virgin nuns, raked the fallen sides
of flaming hedges into tall smouldering piles
that blackened the moon. In the tower room
six women took turns upon a marble throne
until a golem made from frozen blood usurped
their place and played at being king. Exiled
to the steaming lawns they dressed themselves
in black silks and called down starlings from the sky,
took vows of anarchy, hailed a barge made
from smoke, watched one of their number transform
into a fox then skulk off into the shimmering hedgerows.
As night became thick with night
                              the gardeners took their barrows
once again beyond the convent wall where novices
                              cried them full.

In the tower the throne lay empty,
a caking arse-print of blood on its seat. Dark footprints of slush
led their way through the gardens and to the edge
of the canal, its waters muddied red and thickening with ice,
                              the consciousness
of the golem spreading out through the waterways of the city.

Fox

With food I refuse to discriminate:
the river does for me, I need no cup;
the beetle shares its fate with the rabbit,
I separate death from life with one snap.
And more, even on the odd occasion
I have been known to risk the hedgehog's spine.
I am the rancid fire that lights the earth.
I am copper that knows no verdigris.
I steal the newborn from the throes of birth,
I am the farmer's springtime misery.
I root the earthworm from the dripping soil.
Against me nature's force cannot prevail,
as I, drawn by hunger's relentless pull,
tie the deception of night to my tail.

Night

The thin moon squeezes its light
into the darkness of the garden.
Limp blades of montbretia-grass
dream of the burning flowers
that are yet to come.
On the gravelled path snails expand
from the muted trumpet of their shells.
Earwigs unbed themselves
from the tight petals of a rose.
Flies enter the purple vaginas
of digitalis. But she is aware
of none of this, does not know
the names of the flowers, cannot guess
at the urgency of insects,
or indeed that they are urgent,
as she cowers on the wardrobe floor,
her feet half out of the opened
door, her father's drunken kiss
still on her tongue.

the moon's ring fades

she watches from her tower as the moon's ring fades away
and the tides inside her heart begin to slow
nightingales are silent in the gardens of the king
and the creatures in his carpets start to glow
the blankets on her bed are frozen stiff with cold
and a frost is forming on the light-bulb in the room
mold is layered on the walls in crusts of green and grey
and the golden straw is crumbling in the loom
a man on creaking stilts is passing through the town
a sack of sleeping children in his hands
mothers hear sad calling submerged within their dreams
as if ghost-crabs pull them down beneath the sands
Ragged-Nightmare is his name, his hair is made of lead
his coat is made of copper and of tin
his bones are made of limestone
                              and his thoughts are with the dead
and worms weave and gather on his skin
but she watches from her tower as the moon's ring fades away
and the shadows in her cloak slide to the floor
angels shake their wings and free them of their lice
and the rusted doors of heaven move no more

Mice

Stacked beneath the bed my American comics smelled of turpentine.
Their pages crumbled at the edges, scattering bits of Batman
                                    into the bedclothes
each time I opened them up to read. Righteous defender of truth,
the Purple Claw swore his pledge to uphold justice
                                    and fight against evil.
And the four bright angels around my bed, their wings
                                    white in the moonlight,
kept the devil away while I slept. The world is simple
                                    when you're only nine.

High up on the kitchen wall was the electricity meter,
                                    which Dad would feed
with shillings. The meter's brain was a clock, and it ticked benevolently.
But there's no way Dad could get me to feed it a shilling.
                                    I knew what it could do
if it wanted. Some boys who had gone to Saint Joseph's School
had found out for me. They had climbed
                                    inside a transformer box by the canal
and had been filled with light. Mum said
                                    that it was all right in the finish
because they had gone to Heaven. She said that they were helping
the angels look after all the little children
                                    that were still alive in the world.
And I believed her, because the world is simple
                                    when you're only nine.

Each night mice would emerge
                                    from their cities behind the skirting boards.
Crouched on the ground with my ear to the walls, I'd imagine
what their lives were like. You'd hear them
                                    under the floorboards, travelling freely
beneath the house, moving between houses, immune
                                    to surface-dwelling cats.
Dad would sort them though, would spike neat squares of cheese
on tightly sprung traps. I'd check them in the morning,

                    glad when the cheese
was gone, pilfered by the Ghost. That's what I called him, the Ghost.
Already dead, and I knew this as a fact,
                         he couldn't be killed twice. I'd seen him
the morning he'd been caught, his neck snapped beneath the trap.
That very night he'd gone back to work.
                         Weightless, he'd now eat the pale cheese
without springing the bar. Before long, none of the traps
                    were yielding mice,
but the cheese would be gone. Dad reckoned the mice had got smart.
But I knew they'd all been killed,
                         their ghosts now feasting with impunity.

The dead would always outlast the living. The world is simple
                    when you're only nine.

A Japanese Airman Says Goodbye To The War

In the garden   chimes of slices of shell
conjure a song   from the wind.
Amongst the leaves   and fallen blossom
a snail displays   its two-pronged crown.

Mount Fuji   is nothing to this snail
who likewise   is nothing to me.

Your black hair   seems unbearably pure.
I take a tear   as a keepsake.
My plane is screaming   with tongues of fire
but the sea holds me   in its gaze.

The Decline Of The Beetle Empire

The beetle followed a jagged, hesitant route
through the shifting fingers of grass-shadows,
detoured under the immobile shadows of stones.
        Other shadows, unsubstantial, the fast-moving orbs
of feathered seeds, dandelions, hawkweeds,
brushed swiftly over his path.
        Ants pondered in their mathematical courses
as he trundled past them,
ignoring his polished, resplendent body.
        But then a shadow that appeared suddenly
was no longer a shadow, but the piercing sword
of a shrike's beak. And this swift mouth ended,
with one hammering snap,
the secret knowledge of the Beetle Emperor.
        And there was the Beetle Emperor now,
his black cloak crushed,
his delicate petticoats of wings sliced and torn,
and the index of his incredible mind
scattered everywhere.
        A glistening grass-lizard that had observed
all of this
blinked liquidly,
then disappeared as fast as thought,
the long stalks of grass trembling, trembling
where he had been.
        Underneath the ground worms moved blindly
in their tunnels, siphoning the earth
through their long bodies.
        Nearer to the surface, the larvae of beetles
also turned in their gritty womb,
and the tendrils of grass roots
felt their way into the darkness,
grain of earth by grain of earth.

H. G. Wells, two miles from Botley

He'd seen them, black, corybantic: seven horses
                    in a scruffy, ragworty field.

      The wheels of the bicycle
              hummed like bees
              down the last sloping lane,
                    the sun's golden wheel
                        constant in the glass sky.

Yellow-flowered
      Jack-go-to-bed-at-noon
          was up,
              roused at the roadside verge.

He lay the bicycle on its side, wheels turning freely.
          A stalk of grass between his teeth,
          he studied the spokes as the wheels turned,
                  then looked up
                  at the clear
                      cloudless sky.

In the turning wheels he had seen futures:
        cities tumbling through the space
            between stars,
                the moon a wasp-hollowed hive,
                a man who could travel
                ageless through years
                    on a complex velocipede.

Later, cycling through the ribboning road,
        he knew that God was in his head
              thinking the world anew.

Eve

Eve wakes up for the first time
since being expelled
from the Garden of Eden
and realises
that she is the consciousness
of a domestic appliance.
She rises from the bed
but her husband continues to sleep.
She is naked
except for the wedding ring
that her husband
has soldered to her waist.

The serpent
inside the filament
of the electric light-bulb
is awoken as she turns on the light.

I am the light, says Eve.
No, says the serpent.

The serpent
in the dust-bag
is awoken as she plugs in the hoover.

I am the sucking annihilation of the hoover, says Eve.
No, says the serpent.

Then what am I?
You are the wife, says the serpent.
And what do I do?
You tidy up, says the serpent.

Of its own accord the hose uncoils from the hoover.
She begins to hoover her husband.
He is made of ashes and dust
and is drawn up into the hose.

You are the sucking annihilation of the hoover,
says the serpent.
You are the light.

in the streets beneath the ocean

in the streets beneath the ocean
on her coral chair
the fishes whisper secrets
beneath her seaweed hair
she's got a tumour in her head
that's a glowing pearl
she's a strange strange strange
underwater girl

in the streets beneath the ocean
she combs her seaweed hair
the dolphins bring her children
that have drowned down there
and she makes them coats from sailors' skin
gives them gold from sailors' teeth
taken from the sunken ships
wrecked upon the reef

I caught her in a dream one time
or maybe she caught me
took me from my sleeping brain
into the deepest sea
gave me seven kisses
and seven cups of wine
promised me promised me
that she'd be mine

in the streets beneath the ocean
the moon is never seen
it does its work in secret
like an unremembered dream
and all the children dance around
and all the children sing
and the sea queen waits
to see what the sea will bring

in the streets beneath the ocean
on her coral chair
the fishes whisper secrets
beneath her seaweed hair
she's got a tumour in her head
that's a glowing pearl
she's a strange strange strange
underwater girl

The Drowned Sailor

A mermaid dragged me
into the sea
and filled my lungs
with salty water.
Then she tied my feet
with twisting lengths
of slimy seaweed
and anchored me
to the ocean floor.
There she kept me
for seven years
and seven days.
Then she said
"This is what
it feels like
to be taken
from your home.
When you get
back on land,
pass it on."
Then she loosened
my chains of seagrass
and I floated up
through the dark
layers of the sea
until I got caught
in a fisherman's net.
When the fisherman saw
the sea-bloated corpse
that I had now become
he cast me back
into the cold waters
where not even the fish
would eat me.

Eve At The Beach

Between the ocean's troubled tongue
and where the shifting sands begun
she made a man of sand and dung
               and christened him her lover.

"You're just as good as flesh and blood,
my man of excrement and mud,
and when you die in ocean's flood
               I'll build myself another."

girl & the crab-apple moon-cat

a slice of apple
on her tongue
she eats the moon

in her belly
crab-apple moon
becomes a dream

crab-apple moon
pours its light
into the white cat

touching the lake
with its face
cat licks moonlight

silken moon o silken moon
the sleeping child sings
cat hears its name

through the reeds
with its tail up
cat hooks the stars

approaching the yard
cat watches its shadow
cover the house

bulb of paper lantern
moths queue up
for the cat's mouth

through the cat flap
of her dreams
goes the silken moon

Things Are Not Right In The Kingdom

The jester's overcoat
refuses
to leave the wardrobe,
and his shoes,
impatient as always,
have gone on ahead.

Beneath the cankerous
apple tree,
the Knave of Knives
sharpens a spoon.

As the sovereign
rolls beneath
the floorboards
the court mathematician
discovers the concept
of negative numbers.

As the Queen
draws the comb
through her long hair,
she thinks
of dipping spoons
into her husband's body.

In the kitchen
five and twenty mice
have hidden in a cake,
waiting for the cat
to leave the house.

Still in his bed,
asleep,
the King dreams
that he's a playing card.

Someone is holding him
in their grubby fingers.

In the counting house
all the money
deludes itself
that it will never be spent.

The maid is in the garden
hanging out the clothes.
She wipes the Queen's knickers
against her nose.

A Concise Natural History

Shy in their millions the pipistrelle umbrellas
>   Fold themselves away in vast underground wardrobes
>   Hang upside down by a single claw

Often mistaken for metaphors or mythological rainwear
>   Their opened plumage is widely considered unlucky
>   If the sun is under a hundred watts

When battered will invariably display loosened bones
>   And only capable of flight if turned inside out
>   Or shown sideways rain

Known to poke their beaks from those who hold them
>   Underarm while walking backwards in the busy street
>   Useless at golf but useful for it

Black as a rule and often domesticated
>   Their inert shit invisible
>   And not recommended for attic insulation

Reputed to stray
>   And thus often found
>   Riding alone on city buses

The waking of Billery Doo

Billery Doo in his creased raisin coat
slept in his house of cake. His rubbery
snores bub-bubbled to the apricot moat,
and his mumbles from dreams made blueberry
seams erupt in the sugar-iced roof;
and then sparrows and blackbirds ate doorways
and windows, hallways and tunnels enough,
that the house collapsed totally fourways
and Billery Doo awoke with a cough.
"Who was it who tore my house down, right down,
so down it sank in the mud and the rough?"
And blackbirds and sparrows twittered and frowned
and they sang out loud: "Oh Billery Doo,
we've eaten your house, so now we'll eat you."

Tea with Akhmatova's cat

I'm having tea with Akhmatova's cat
who purrs in English passable enough
that half-wit mice can follow what she's at.

She speaks in metres forcible but flat:
a mix of Milton, Keats, hairballs and fluff.
I'm having tea with Akhmatova's cat.

Quite bored, I count the fibres on the mat,
pretend I'm listening, fake attention, cough.
The half-wit mice can follow what she's at.

Her ginger body trembles in its fat,
remembers pogroms, deaths, and other stuff.
I'm having tea with Akhmatova's cat.

The truth is, I'm not worthy of her chat,
miss the point, even though it's not so tough
that half-wit mice can't follow what she's at.

The cat consumes the mouse and that is that;
in canine jaws the cat will know its worth.
I'm having tea with Akhmatova's cat;
the half-wit mice can follow what she's at.

The Witch

With a laugh like a clattering shutter
the magpie flew into the bedroom, knocked
bottles of perfume from off the dresser,
scattered her underwear all over, picked
one fine golden ring from out of its box,
then out through the billowing curtains, out
into the trees that had escaped the axe,
the border of willow yet to be cut,
and flinging the ring straight into its craw
began to shout like a jester gone wild.
So when she came wet from the bath and saw
the perfume spilling from jars, the unpiled
clothes and mess, she slipped the latch of her tongue
and cursed the bird, who withered bone by bone.

thief of dreams

I found her at the base
of the twisting stairs,
painting the steps
with discarded rain.
I found her at night
counting my dreams,
counting my dreams
and repeating my name.
I found her in the garden
hanging the wings
of butterflies
on the washing-line.
"Take off your skin
and I'll mend it," she said
But then a raven
unfolded itself
from her black hair,
and before I could say
yes or no
I was no longer there.

Somewhere else was a darkened room. A candle was guttering and
the light was fading. The stems of three rushes were lying on the
table. Next to the rushes was a long vase containing hot wax. I
dipped the rushes into the wax, and then lit the ends on the last
breath of the extinguishing candle. By the smokey light of the rushes
I made my way through a winding corridor. Eventually I came to
another room. An unlit candle was on the table, and as I picked it up
I could see that it was a perfect waxen effigy of myself, the white
virgin wick poking up through the top of my head. As the rushes
began to falter I lit the candle. Immediately my whole body became
warm and someone called my name. Then a raven unfolded itself
from the darkness of the room, and before I could say yes or no I
was somewhere else.

Her fine little men

Locked out, the moon is barely a pale slit.
Mamma Quince's candles are the colour
of raw silk. Small imperfections like grit
run through the wax, shine at the wick's waver:
the jagged crushed remnants of broken teeth,
scattered millimetre-snips of blond hair,
an infant's finger-nail clipping, skin-breadth
of skin, eye-lashes woven in a square.
And as the melted wax curls down, down
the diminishing candles, it assumes
the shapes of men. Men paler than the moon,
stiff dollkins, all of them the size of thumbs;
her fetish-charms birthed of human debris,
translucent soldiers, her own toy army.

ballad of the heir to darkness

all I found on my father's chair
were the death's head moths that rested there
a faded stain from the quartered moon
and the taste of honey on a spoon

as I sat down the moths came out
and settled on me like a coat
a coat of grey with many skulls
the type the devils wear in hell

and clothed in this I stepped outside
and found a blood-red horse to ride
and took him down through the airless clay
where my dead rotting father lay

and on his corpse was a bloom of mould
and round his head a crown of gold
and through his chest a twisted horn
the headpiece from a unicorn

I unscrewed the horn that pierced him dead
put the crown of gold upon my head
and galloped to the sleeping town
the sunrise shining on my crown

"I wear a coat of death's head moths
and ride a steed as red as blood
I take my place in my father's stead
as Lord of the Living and the Dead"

for all I found on my father's chair
were the death's head moths that rested there
a faded stain from the quartered moon
and the taste of honey on a spoon

up and down in their sleep

One night the snakes-and-ladders board woke up
while the whole house slept. Ladders clattered down
the stairs, set themselves up against walls, climbed
to nowhere but themselves. Serpents entered
through opened doors, folded themselves neatly
into cupboards. One, coiled into the bath,

filled it to the brim with his bulk. The bath
tap dripped on the snake's head as it looked up
at each descending drop. Then, mice entered
every room from behind the skirting, climbed
up the tails of snakes, turned round, climbed back down.
In their hundreds mice assembled neatly

on the backs of snakes, with sharp teeth neatly
slit the skin from every one. In the bath
the snake suddenly found his time was up,
likewise every snake in the house entered
the outside with its insides. Earwigs climbed
from behind their dark spaces and looked down

at the coils of red meat. Bright blood soaked down
into the carpets, across tiles, neatly
filled, (a crimson pool), the enamelled bath.
Meanwhile, the grating of ladders woke up
the youngest child. On tiptoe he entered
his parent's room, toes sticky with blood, climbed

into their bed and fell fast asleep; climbed
straight back into a dream where he fell down
the back of a snake. Three squares further up
a wooden ladder leant against the bath.
Down at his feet the number five neatly
filled the square in which he stood. Mice entered

the square and scurried up his legs, entered

his pyjamas, nibbled at his skin, climbed
down his legs again. They'd slit his skin down
from his head to his toes. It slipped neatly
from his body. "I'm a walking bloodbath",
he thought to himself before waking up

in his parent's bed. He sat up, entered
day. Sunlight filtered down; deep shadows climbed
walls, neatly filled curtain folds, gaps, the bath......

an encounter with the seventh prince

for Gabriel Rosenstock

the rain has deepened
the colour of his raincoat
to that of a hen's egg

the grey clouds slip
from the lens
of his glasses

his pockets are stuffed
with the flattened bodies
of animals he's pulled
from the road
          hedgehogs, badgers, foxes, cats

the moon is caught
in the curls of his head

he speaks five languages at once
commands starlings to shift
the sky from place to place

he catches sight of me
malingering at the edge
of the lake

I'm making a coat
of grass
which I'll wear
as I open the green door
of my neighbour's pond

it's my plan to rescue
the frogs and the fishes there

he sees what I'm about

approaches

he chides me
for wanting to change
the pain of others

tells me instead
to learn the quiet phrase
the nine words that will still the sea
sever the clouds from the sky

the dirt in his nail
coagulates
into a blackbird

sings seventeen
syllables of song

and my tongue
is suddenly anointed
with the gift
of sense

Uncle Jack

Coming up the rutted drive to the yard with a roguish grin on his face
I knew he had something got for me

For one time he'd got me a drum, a cowboy gun
once he'd opened a furze bush to let loose linnets, finches, wrans
laughed as he'd lied he'd made them appear
out of nothing

So here he was now, come into the yard

"I've brought some money from the sea," he said
and pulled a stained, crumpled
brown paper bag
from out of his pocket

and poured
black snails, black snails the size of sixpences, dozens of them

He took a pin from his lapel and began to prick out the creature
from the shell

The thing looked like snot coming from a tiny black nose

and then he put it to his mouth and ate it

I looked at him in wonder, couldn't believe
just couldn't believe that my Uncle Jack had just eaten a snail
had just eaten a snail that looked like a snot

"Now, ye try it," he said.

He'd never let me down,
had got me a drum, a cowboy gun, could magic up birds as quick
                        as you please,
so I did it

I let Uncle Jack put a pin-prick of snail to my mouth
and I ate it

We sat in the yard and finished the bag
the Easter sky vibrant above our heads
the taste of the sea on our tongues

Sat in the yard
like two sea-princes stranded miles inland
our mouths rich with creatures of snot
the black empty shells of our fortune
spent at our feet

grandmother, grandmother

Granny Curtin, my maternal grandmother, lived with my granda on a farm in Brosna, in County Kerry. We'd travel over the sea from England to visit every summer, and then, as the summer waned, we'd journey back to the autumn rains of London. On the night she died my kid brother Gerard ran into my parent's room because there was an old woman standing beside his bed. Instantly, my mother knew that the old woman was her own mother, come to say goodbye. This very same moment I had awoken to Gerard's voice coming from my parent's room; awoken, as it happens, from a dream of my granny walking back to Ireland beneath the sea, clouds of sea-mud rising from her footfalls. That same day my granda told his grieving family he'd be leaving as well, and they told him to shush and not to be foolish. Later the next morning granda suffered a massive heart attack and fell in the yard. We needed no doctor to tell us he'd died of a broken heart. So granda and granny Curtin died and were buried side by side the very same week.

asleep my head cut by stars I hold tight her grey hair skywards

Granny Sexton, my paternal grandmother, lived on a farm in Templeglantine, in County Limerick. Grandad Sexton was a handsome, no-nonsense man who had spent years in New York as a cop before returning home to Ireland. He farmed the land and kept cattle and walked on hard nails. I remember him as being authoritative and gruff. By all accounts granny Sexton was the proverbial saint, always saying her prayers. Apparently, when I was a young boy I would sit beside her keeping her company, and we would pray for the safety of the whole world; but I have no memory of this. The only clear memory I have is of her sitting up in her hospital bed with a black rosary in her hands. Her hair was as white as her nightdress, and an oblong of sunlight was thrown over her bed like an extra sheet.

thrush song fills the window her papery skin throws light at the sun

the thinking hill asleep

The moon with a bite taken out of it
sits lopsided in the cold sky, white stars
smeared up there too, far too high to effect
the horses deep as shadows sleeping fast
in the frosted fields. In the horses' heads
dreams beyond the callous calculations
of astronomy, beyond the knowledge
of men or women, even beyond those
who during the day rode upon their backs
through the rise of grass, the same hill asleep
and dreaming them all into its earthy
skull. Dreaming the horses still as statues,
dreaming the trees breathing through solid lungs,
dreaming the houses digesting their meals
of the excreted dreams of householders.

Sixfaces and the Woman of Nothing

Sixfaces is asleep in the grass, all of his eyes
closed at once. He has been asleep for so long
that the grasses have begun to take root in his mind.
Two lovers enter one of his mouths and begin to couple
on his tongue. Bats have entered at his twelve ears,
their excrement layered night after night.
Sixfaces is dreaming six times over, six different dreams.
His six-sided brain is throbbing with thought,
but he'll remember not one single thing.

A woman of nothing finds him lying asleep.
She has never seen anything so curious before,
a wheel of six faces. She would lift it but she has no hands,
gently toe it over the grass but she has no feet. She'd kiss
the six mouths one by one but she has no mouth of her own.
House Martens emerge from his twelve nostrils,
catch insects in flight and then return. Bees
have built their hives in the ducts at the corners of his eyes.

How beautiful he is, fast asleep. Wild pigs emerge
from one of his mouths, go rooting amongst the trees.
Monkeys scramble up the lines of his foreheads,
disappear into his thick hair. *Wake up, wake up,*
thinks the woman of nothing, but her thoughts are soundless.
She lies down beside him, begins to doze. Soon she is asleep,
her nothing head dreaming of nothing. She becomes the space
that he'll see if he wakes.

Charon

A white detergent bottle, its skin bleached by the sea,
gives off a dull light against the darker stones.
The moon looks down, its flesh bright, its lips dumb.
Water is rustling against the beach
but she isn't listening. She undresses completely,
her body cold in the night air.
Colder she becomes as slowly she dresses
her body with the sea. Forty feet out
she treads water, hearing for the first time
the sea against the shore. With her left arm paddling
she rudders herself till she is facing
the open darkness, away from land. She has to wait
only a few minutes before it comes.
She can feel the water trembling against her flesh.
Sea suddenly unfolds, cut open by its long
bottle snout. Rising out of its liquid earth
it circles her, standing upright on its tail,
the sea commanded by its will
to set like stone. Then water becomes water
once more, and it slips inside.
She takes hold of its fin and it carries her,
joyously, triumphantly, into the space between lives.

seven eyes nine eyes twelve

lamprey mouth their language of scars
seven eyes nine eyes twelve
tissued flesh their face of knives
seven eyes nine eyes twelve

lamps ray south their coinage of stars
seven eyes nine eyes twelve
lighthouse cyclops sheds its tears
seven eyes nine eyes twelve

lamps spray forth their carnage of shards
seven eyes nine eyes twelve
ships pass down through fathomless years
seven eyes nine eyes twelve

Oisín

He remembered the sweet smell of apples
rotting in the grass, the gentle footsteps
of a beetle across his face, the bud
of her nipple, the shadows of grass-stalks
against her flesh, her lips that leant to kiss,
and all in the moment that the saddle
slipped, throwing him against the beckoning earth,
that called him to join with the rotting fruit,
the slow dance of beetles through soil and grit,
the grasses taking root against his skin,
and the freshly dug grave that knew his name.

night work

The dead sailor's mother sits in a pool of light
seeping from the oil-lamp. The linen she embroiders
is stained with the ghosts of tears long soaked
into the slubbed surface she holds in her hands.
With care she guides a needle through the cloth,
its shining body pulling a tail of bright thread.
Tonight she fashions a sun that shimmers down
on bluebirds. They dance through the dirty shapes
left by her fallen tears. Frogs darker than the grass
they inhabit croak noiselessly, for this picture
has no life. The sun finished, she knots
the yellow thread and snips it with her scissors.
A moth, suddenly disturbed as she shakes the cloth,
flits up to the body of the lamp, lands
on the glass funnel and sizzles into nothing.

Ferment

The apples in the bowl
are beginning to shrivel.
As I slice them into quarters,
and then into eighths,
I can see the soft, bruising cancers
spreading through dimming flesh.

Crossing the slope that falls
to the wet fields by the river,
I pass spears of daffodils,
their unborn flowers
still folded tight
into their long heads.
At the fence I click my tongue;
the pony turns from its nosing
among sodden rushes.
Seeing the fractions of apples
piled in my hands,
he moves steadily from the river,
his head nodding as he canters over.
His coat is smeared with mud,
his eyes thick with syrupy tears.
He eats the apples that I have scattered,
their flesh as rancid as fermenting grass.
When he is finished he turns to the river,
his hooves cutting into the earth,
the whole field where he is
churned at his feet.

A lethargic drizzle
is settling down
from the dead sky.

The smudged woman in the willow-pattern

indistinct, a ghost of troubled form
the princess treads upon the bridge

in the distance an old man
stands on a creaking raft

overhead the blue swallows accumulate
they shit indiscriminately

everything is blue except the sky
which is white
and the depths of the river
which are white

nothing will ever move here
no one will ever reach a destination
the swallows are as stationary
as the stars
appear one by one as you look up
but always in the same place
like the stars

a man is fishing from a wooden pier
has been there forever
and will remain forever
and will catch nothing

a pagoda stands
surrounded by blossoming plum trees
its solid blue door closed
so that nothing can enter or leave

everything is blue except the sky
which is white
and the depths of the river
which are white
and the shit falling indiscriminately
from the swallows

which are blue

everything is blue

the gardener's heart

As green as green as the gardener's heart
are the pampered lawns of the sterile park
where autumn's rot is yet to start

From the clogged canal sounds the barge's blart
in waters fetid with algae dark
and green as green as the gardener's heart

In the sally wood brays the wounded hart
the echoing trumpet and savage bark
where autumn's rot is yet to start

A witch picks nightshade for a nightshade tart
entered in ledgers by the witch's clerk
in ink as green as the gardener's heart

A playful child throws a barley dart
the starlings bicker in their swooping arc
and autumn's rot is yet to start

The ruined admiral dreams of his chart
as he sleeps in the hedge with a preening lark
and green as green is the gardener's heart
as autumn's rot is yet to start

Deirdre to Conchobhar

While the gold furze was breaking from the bud
I slipped the moorings of my mother's womb;
and as the midwife wiped me clean of blood,
a royal visitor proclaimed my doom.
Oh cruel King, I was a child just born.
Why did you have to take me to your heart,
and to my beauty cast your ancient worm,
and nurture in me fifteen years of hate?
When I died, my head split upon a rock,
it's said my soul resprouted in the soil
and in that way outlived your earthly work.
The hammer was defeated by the nail.
Men will talk for centuries of your lust,
and by that talk you'll be forever cursed.

The Garden

The lawn wakes from a dream
of someone trimming his hair.
But now that he is awake
his hair is long, falling
carelessly under its own weight.
Beetles tickle his skin; they
have discovered the body
of a blackbird beneath a shrub.
The lawn watches passively
as the beetles strip the bones
of flesh. The lawn imagines
that he is clothing the naked
bones of the blackbird
with grass, taking the fine
skeletal wings into his own being.
Asleep, the lawn dreams of flight.

The green owl

In class on Tuesday she draws a picture for Mrs Grey
and gets two gold stars. It's a picture of a house inside the moon
Inside the chimney of the house is a badger, his snout pointing up
and inside the walls of the house are mice running up and down
and she's drawn herself inside a fishbowl with a single goldfish
and she's wearing a dress that's covered in ladybirds
and the goldfish is kissing her kissing her

She brings the picture home with her and mammy pins it up
She's in her bed now looking at the picture through moonlight
Daddy's shouts move through the walls, tremble the carpet of her room
She gets out of bed and stands on the carpet to keep them down
Outside in the dark an owl says who

With half its face bright in the tall sky
                        the moon's face is half black like mammy's
Night by night she's been watching the moon bruising in the tall sky

On Wednesday for Mrs Grey she makes a green owl from plasticine
and gets two gold stars. The green owl has big goggles on
and its goggles catch and store moonlight,
                        and moonbeams can come from its eyes
Night by night she's going to watch
                        the moon's face heal in the tall bright sky
watch the moon's face become white like mammy's

On Thursday she falls asleep in class, her head resting on her desk
She dreams of the green owl and it carries her and mammy to the moon
It's lashing wet as they fly through the sky
and a train shouts who through the driving rain
and they come to a house with mice in the walls
and a badger breathes smoke through the chimney
and mammy puts her safely in a fishbowl
                        and a single goldfish kisses her kisses her
and Mrs Grey gives her two gold stars

Night Cats

Night hides cats that jump to the shadows night wears,
preen demurely out of the sight of windows,
balance on the tongue of the moon if light is
                                        burning the darkness.

Cats eat mice that stray out of leaf-earth, impale
birds with claws that shatter the hedgehog's kingdom,
rustle beetles whirring through ink-thick dreams of
                                        God. Is what night is.

the old man in the pond

His beard is five rough strings of gristled skin
falling beneath his lip. Bloated leaches
breathe the secrets of his blood; blood engine
thumping in the tightly layered reaches
within him. An army of lice itches
his scaled hull. He is the ancient of mud,
and though blind as mud his dull eye etches
the murk with his will, all the rotting dead
sediment the single signal in his head.
Way down here in the soft slop of decay
the pale flesh of the emperors has shed
like their clothes. Finger rings have slipped away
into the dark, no brighter than a bone.
In this his black hell he is lord alone.

invocation of intercession to the earthly angels

magpie	over the darkened river	pray for them
fox	hidden in the reeds	pray for them
crow	finding the shape of the wind	pray for them
snail	in your tunnel of self	pray for them
grass	in your infinite bodies	pray for them
whale	in your palace of water	pray for them
pebble	in your shouldering nations	pray for them
worm	filtering the endless earth	pray for them

A Letter to My Other

we have never met except in dreams
and although you take many forms
I have always known it is you

once you appeared before me
in a thin golden mask
your red hair burning like the sun

and many times you take the form
of enormous insects, but I always know
it is you

and even those times
when you have appeared as a woman
and we have kissed

I have always known it is you
and always, always in those many dreams
when you call me by my name

I know it is you

Rhyme for the inside of cupboards

moleman moves through his tunnel of worms
and the ground gives way beneath his push
and when he sleeps in his tightening bed
he dreams he dreams of the darkest earth

the owl is wrapped in his feathered cloak
the air awaits his merciless touch
his thoughts the earth and its fecund mulch
surrendering mice of their trembling flesh

moleman moves through his tunnel of worms
and the ground gives way beneath his push
and when he sleeps in his tightening bed
he dreams he dreams of the darkest earth

the owl is wrapped in his feathered cloak
the air awaits his merciless touch
his thoughts the earth and its fecund mulch
surrendering mice of their trembling flesh

the wilding apple

the wilding apple leans by the shore
its ten sour children fall into the sea

one is snatched from the pebbled strand
a grey rook splits it on a stone
one is let to sail the waves
its head bob-bobbing all alone

the wilding apple leans by the shore
its ten sour children fall into the sea

one is as green as the sea itself
as green as sea-grass in the tides
one is as black as the sea itself
its cankered skin its calm flesh hides

the wilding apple leans by the shore
its ten sour children fall into the sea

one is lifted by a child
leaning from the village pier
one is eaten by a widow
its bitterness draws a tear

the wilding apple leans by the shore
its ten sour children fall into the sea

one I open with a knife
count its piplets one by one
one I open with my teeth
its acrid secrets tell my tongue

the wilding apple leans by the shore
its ten sour children fall into the sea

one has flesh as pale as yours

its piplets dark as night
one is home to the codling worm
its flesh as pale as light

the wilding apple leans by the shore
its ten sour children fall into the sea

The final years of King Canute

inside a half-filled beerglass he keeps the sea
it sits impotently on the mantelpiece where it is largely forgotten
the lady who cleans the house has been told to ignore it
she no longer sees it, it no longer bothers her
it is just a half-filled beerglass clogged with thick sludge
sometimes someone will pass a remark, wonder what it is
he just says it's the sea, he trapped it there years ago
that liquid that fills the basins of the earth is an impostor
the sea has been here in this glass for years
the lady who cleans the house wanted to throw it away
but he keeps it to remind him of how powerful he once was

the lost-and-found office of your heart

I bring
the parings of the moon
        to your door
all the abandoned waves
        of the sea
the unmeltable shadows
        of snowmen
the afterthoughts
        of autumn leaves
the tunnellings
        of moles
all the lost, the left-behind
        the forgotten
the in and of and out
        of all that is gone

and trust
        that under your care
                they will be glorified
and I can bathe
        in their transcendent
                light

The two rooms

The black-haired girl is inside her blue room
She paints an eye on the wall and looks through
Through the eye there are no restrictions
For the eye in her room is better than a telescope
She adjusts her gaze to a distant place
There's someone inside a white dusty room
He's painted an enormous ear on his wall
He is leaning up against it and listening
She does not realise that he is listening to her heartbeat
He's been listening to it for months, fascinated
She watches him for a long time, falls in love with him
He notices that her heart is changing rhythm
It's faster than usual and the sound entrances him
She watches him, rapt in his listening
He seems so happy and she wishes she could be the same
Just by watching him she gets that way as well
She spends an hour looking at him through the eye
                    in her blue room
In his white dusty room he listens for the variations of her heart

like...

like a small boy who thinks that letting fog
seep into the house (down the corridor
and up the stairs to fill all the bedrooms)
will raise the house up into the sky as
soon as the fog lifts, I breathe whispered words
into your ear, knowing that when I go
you'll be tethered to my leaving, will rise
with me up the cloud stairway to my house
of rain, where we'll cross the silver threshold
into a dazzling room of noising light

My Father's Acre

with big freckles
two-tone mapped
eating the grass
 are black and white cows

slow glances
 are all
we will get
 except indifference

as though
 they know everything
the grass
 tells them

the grass
whose blood
 cows hold
drunk by us

For the garden path he'd promised her

For the garden path he'd promised her
my father bought eight yards of sand.
My mother watched the lorry pour
its hissing load of brittle cloud
and all the neighbours gathered round
and wondered what would come about;
oh kings of gold and grit we were
as we played upon that yellow mound.
For weeks it stood before the house
taking up the space of cars;
summer evenings it steamed with rain,
changed its hues from brown to straw,
filled our fingernails with grain
and shaped our footprints on the floor.
As it strayed throughout the house
mum would gather it in the pan
take it back to its troubled heap
where it could wander yet again.
The wind would tempt it to the air
with Jerusalems of other streets
but mother brushed its drifting tides
and tamed it to the roadside curb.
The weekend came when dad split bags
of cement grey as graveyard stones
and in that day of burning sun
our mother watched her path begin.
We made a lid for the kitchen yard
smothered thistles in their thoughts
and under mother's silent guard
we laid a walkway through the lawn.
That evening red as pots of jam
we bore our sunburnt backs to mum
who soothed them cold with calamine
and told us we were her best men.

For the garden path he'd promised her
my father bought eight yards of sand.

song

I leave a kiss within this clasp
that's shaped in silver like a wasp,
then place it firmly in your grasp:
                    In darkness it will grow.

And it will fester into love,
defy below and all above,
and whatever we are thinking of
                    each one shall always know.

a vision found on a classroom wall

she lifted up a corner of the sea   and pulled
                              up it came under her grip   up   up
she robed herself in it   robed herself in it because she was naked
but now the sea   fell about her body   in thick folds
fish moved in and out   of this robe   invisible one moment
                              lost beneath the depths
visible another   on the surface of the robe   like a pattern   then gone
whales   as small to her   as beetles   congregated   at her hemline

over her head   she placed   twelve   enormous   clam shells
each clam the size of a mountain
each clam   as golden   as a star

the sun   pregnant with fire   gave birth to a child
                              his body swaddled   in yellow light
and she caught up the child   as it fell   towards the earth
and held it close   in her arms

the child touched her breast   and
at his touch   her breast was clothed   in the same light
                              that swaddled him
the light sank   beneath her robe   lit up the deep
                              ocean of her cloak   from within

on the dry seafloor   she found a key   that fitted exactly
                              into the lock   of heaven

falling apart, making up

a man made of coins was spent by his wife
for angel's wings and a very sharp knife
she cut some cabbage just for the devil
and made him soup she stirred with a shovel
meanwhile her husband was counted in hell
all of his pieces until he was well
he climbed a ladder right up to the ground
and went home to his wife, each penny sound
he stole her wings and flew over the town
got struck by lightning: each penny fell down
she picked him up and put him together
penny by penny, feather by feather

Mantra Of The Awoken Powers

in a copse of blackthorn he cut a stave
then went beside my heart where I never went
then saw the place I was in that I never saw
then heard the songs I sang that I never heard
then said the words I spoke that I never said
and by a rocky shore he trapped a fish
then came to the mind where I never came
then thought the thoughts I thought that I never thought
then made the promises I made that I never made
then broke the hearts I broke that I never broke
then kissed the lips I kissed that I never kissed
and in a bush of furze he caught a bird
then fell into the soul where I never fell
then killed the hope I killed that I never killed
then breathed the breath I breathed that I never breathed
then weaned the child I weaned that I never weaned
then lost the self I lost that I never lost

and in my hand I held a stave
and in my mouth I held a fish
and with my foot I held a bird
and I was alive though he was dead
and I moved though he was still

and I remain though he remaineth not

I can see you

her voice drifting from an opened window
I hear Mum calling my name
opening the wardrobe to see
if I have become a coat

and out in the back Dad is balanced
over the top of the tall galvanized fence
looking down into the ragwort-clotted artery of the alley
but I'm nowhere, I've disappeared

crouched beneath the privet hedge
of the front garden
I am invisible
as invisible as the thrush

the earwigs that drop into my hair
the hidden undersides of leaves
the uncertain filtered light
no one will ever find me

John, are you there?
where are you John?   John
for the first time
I can feel my name

as solid as I am
yet as elusive

beneath the privet hedge
I waver in leaf-light

Song of Taliesin

I was the work which Nimrod oversaw.
I witnessed the destruction of Sodom and Gomorrah.
I was at the court of Dôn before Gwydion's birth;
At the White Hill my head lies under the earth;
it is not known if I am flesh or fish.
I was at the Crucifixion with Mary Magdala.
I was the banner carried before Alexander.
I strengthened Moses in the land of the Name.
I was in Canaan when Absalom was slain.
I was chief bard to the prisoner Elphin.
I was the child whose name was Gwion;
my brain was inflamed by Cerridwen's cauldron.
Cerridwen swallowed me and carried my foetus;
I have been John, Merlin the Wise, the prophet Elias.
Become I Taliesin, Teacher to the Universe.
I was with my Lord in the Highest Sphere,
then curled me up upon His floor.
I carried the Muse across the Jordan,
conveyed the Spirit to the Vale of Hebron.
I was the Throne of the Distributor;
to the Danes of Lochlin I was chief singer.
In the Ark I was fostered and am the Great Teacher.
I have been in India and Asia,
but come now to the remnant of Troia.
I have sat for nights in an uneasy chair,
and named the stars through Heaven's hair;
from the land of the Cherubim I brought me there.
I stood on the firmament of the unsteady ocean,
and have mastered movement without any motion.
Before I had speech I was never dumb;
I am Alpha Tetragrammaton.
I was with Jesus and the Ass upon the straw.
I fell through the Heavens with Lucifer;
I was instructor to Enoch and Noah,
with Enoch and Elias I grasped the tail.
With the Son of the Virgin I suffered the Nail,
hung on the cross inside his Mantle
and was three times inside the Spiral Castle.
I am a wonder whose origin has not begun,
and shall remain upon the earth until all is done.

The Goddess of Merciless Love

There are three apprenticeships that a poet should serve. The first is the apprenticeship to Life, which everyone should serve anyway, whether they're a poet or not. However, as in any pursuit, it may be served well or badly or not at all. The second apprenticeship is the apprenticeship to the Craft of Poetry. Now, there are many poets who fail to serve this apprenticeship in any way, although the truth is, it's never too late to serve, because it has no end: You'll be serving it till the day they stick you down the hole. The third apprenticeship is the apprenticeship to Despair. Unlike the other two, this one isn't optional. Everyone gets to serve this one.

Despair can be in large things, or it can be in small things. You place your poems into little brown envelopes, and send them, little brown envelope by little brown envelope, to complete strangers. Then you wait for envelopes to come back. The ones that come to you might contain your poems, unwanted. You wait for them, hoping for a magnificent letter of acceptance, knowing that you may be getting a shitty little letter of rejection, and realising that you'll settle for a magnificent letter of rejection. Sometimes you can get a shitty little letter of acceptance. I got one of those the other day, from Poetry Scotland. They want one of my poems, but the letter looks as if it's been written on toilet paper. This is what you get for dedicating your life to poetry.

In order to cope with the despair poets have sought comfort in a concept. Some people call this concept the Muse. And there are many poets who see her as a woman, a goddess. She is beautiful or ugly, depending on her mood. She is young or old, depending on her mood. She is loving or hateful, depending on her mood.

On a Monday she will give you her breasts to suckle. On a Tuesday she will piss on your head. On a Wednesday she will bare your children. On a Thursday she will give you the Flu. On a Friday your milk will flow to the brim, and you'll have maggots in your cheese. Saturday is a day sacred to her. Sunday is a day profane to her. And on these two days she will do whatever is in her mind to do.

Now, there are some poets who follow a different muse, a male one. Their muse has golden hair and the scent of a rutting stag. He also has the most magnificent penis imaginable. He will fill your head with ideas and your tongue will overflow with language. He will fill your head with ideas and your tongue with language *not* because he cares about ideas, *not* because he cares about language, and certainly not because he cares about you, but simply because he's full of juice.

The goddess *only* cares about language. She only cares about the expression of ideas through language. But if you are a woman, she will give you a sisterly affection. If you are a woman she will give you a motherly affection. If you are a man she will give you affection in other ways. But she is a harsh mistress. And I know.

You dedicate your life to Her. You serve Her unremittingly. You love no one but Her. Only to discover that she's knocking about with every other poet in the country. But whatever her attributes, and whatever her vices, thankfully She has an Infinite sense of humour.

Of course, there are many poets who do not consciously follow any muse whatsoever. To them, the concept of the muse is a subjective invention. And quite frankly, to argue the point would be a waste of time, because first-hand knowledge of the muse is usually dependant on personal experience, which is *always* subjective.

I first became aware of the Muse as a child. In the beginning, being only four or five and not having much experience in such matters, I simply thought that the woman's voice in my head belonged to my maternal grandmother. It was only as I got a bit older that I realised that it couldn't possibly be my grandmother as she lived in Kerry and at that time we were living in London. But at the age of four or five I had simply and naively assumed that that's how grannies communicated with people. As a voice in one's mind.

The strange thing about this woman's voice was that it never really said anything of consequence, although on the very rare occasion I do recall being told off. Even to this day I can't quite remember what for. As I got older the voice became less frequent. These days I rarely hear her at all.

But although her voice has gone, she often appears in

dreams. Once she stood before me in a thin golden mask, her hair made of fire, but many times she takes the guise of enormous insects, mainly dragonflies but sometimes beetles.

Once, after a conversation with an acquantainance concerning the Muse, this person had a dream. She 'phoned me the following evening and told me about it. We were in a room together, the room totally sealed and without windows, and we were surrounded by a kind of muggy darkness. My friend was on one side of the room, standing on her own, and I was kneeling down on the other side, with my head bowed. As my friend watched, the room was filled with light, and as she looked she could see that the light was pouring out of a woman who was approaching me with a basin of water. As the woman came upon me she poured the entire contents over my head. At this point something within the context of the dream itself allowed my friend to realise that the woman was the Muse and that I had been anointed. On waking the following morning, my friend felt a certain degree of jealousy that she had been ignored. I pointed out to her that we had both been in the same room. The only difference between us was that my friend was standing and I was kneeling. One must always kneel before the Muse.

However, the truth is that these days I experience the Muse largely as a burning conviction that she exists. It is simply an act of faith. But what degree of faith I cannot honestly say. I simply do not dare to disbelieve in her. What poet could?

silence

she could hear grass
expanding from its roots
pushing its many tongues through the soil
she could hear worms
turning through the earth
the squeak of their skin
revolving through mud
she could hear debates
in the minds of ants
the parliaments of bees and wasps
she could hear the foetus
forming in the yolk of the egg
she could even hear stars
being formed in distant space
infinities before she herself was formed
their energies curdling into flames
and she could hear
quite distinctly
the catch in her father's breath
as he found her dead
on the kitchen floor

Praise for John W. Sexton's previous book *Vortex*

There is a sense in which John W. Sexton's impressive third collection is not so much about the "possibilities of place" as displacement...... Sexton's way of exploring the "space inside" is what makes him different and unusual. It is what gives this collection depth, insight, honesty, and humour. He displays examples of fine poetic craft in his use of allegory, fantasy, mantra-like repetition, and in the sonnet and ballad forms. Amongst the most refreshing things about this collection is that Sexton emerges as his own man, clearly standing apart from trends towards obscurity and self-consciousness that fuel the work of his contemporaries. *Vortex* you will not forget. John W. Sexton the poet is building for himself a lovely relationship with his readers. **John Doorty, The Stony Thursday Book**

Vortex is a world of contrasts, where meaning is telescoped to the reader precisely; where there is cinematic clarity in the landscapes, mindscapes and soundscapes that John W. Sexton photographs for us.......This collection presents us with snapshots of thought from a poet who feels deep emotion, deep conflict and deep meaning. **Patrick Boyle, The Stinging Fly**

Approaching the fine edge of madness and an outstanding read. **Gary Blankenship, Loch Raven Review**

...a powerful collection suffused with the tangled emotions of relationships, memory, and loss. But there's joy in it as well, a kind of daredevil revelling in the beauty of the unknown, in the myriad possibilities that life offers. It's clear that Sexton embraces life. **Laurie Seidler, VerbSap.**

Sexton's own sure hand with poetic craft is extraordinary, and he's not afraid to put it to use, whether for delicate lyrics or for horror. Highly recommended. **Dr. Suzette Haden Elgin (The Linguistics & Science Fiction Newsletter)**

Remarkable remintings of the dark fantasy inherent in much folktale and song and its abiding archetypal intrusion into our surface modernity in stress. **Steve Sneyd (Data Dump #90)**

Here are poems that carefully dissect the careless cruelty of life...... This collection is powerful stuff that works both emotionally and intellectually and repays re-reading. **Juliet Wilson, New Hope International**

There are signs of Irish magic realism aplenty in John W. Sexton's *Vortex*.....whose bizarre leaps of the imagination and left-field thoughts spoke to me most forcefully. **Fiona Curran, Orbis**

Other Works by John W. Sexton

POETRY

The Prince's Brief Career (*Cairn, 1996*)
Shadows Bloom / **Scáthanna Faoi Bhláth** (*Doghouse, 2004*)
Vortex (*Doghouse, 2005*)

NOVELS FOR CHILDREN

The Johnny Coffin Diaries (*The O'Brien Press, 2001*)
Johnny Coffin School-Dazed (*The O'Brien Press, 2002*)

OTHER MEDIA:

CD

Sons of Shiva (*Track Records, 2003*)

RADIO

The Ivory Tower (*RTE Radio 1, 1999 – 2002*)